S0-BOF-056

The Young Children's Encyclopedia

Volume 14

Printed in the U.S.A.
Library of Congress Catalog Card Number: 76-41025
International Standard Book Number: 0-85229-322-4

Encyclopædia Britannica, Inc.

Chicago
London
Toronto
Geneva
Sydney
Tokyo
Manila
Seoul

Table of Contents Volume 14

Here are more words beginning with "S" . . . *and* . . . **Here is where you may read about them**

The Fish That Go Up Waterfalls

These fish aren't going down a waterfall. They're going *up!*

Nothing can stop these big, strong salmon. Not even a waterfall pouring down on them can make them turn back. The water smashes and splashes, but the salmon flip, wriggle, and twist, finally going up and over the waterfall in great leaps.

Even then they don't stop to rest. They keep on swimming *up* the river, while the water rushes *down* on its long way from the mountains to the ocean.

Where are the salmon going?

The salmon are swimming up the river to return to the quiet waters where they were hatched. They started far out in the ocean—too far away to see land anywhere.

But somehow the salmon find the land. They even find the particular river that they are looking for. Night and day they swim on, almost never stopping to eat or rest.

The salmon swim past cities and towns and farms and forests. They often have to get away from fishermen . . . and sometimes from bears. They swim under bridges and around dams and leap over high waterfalls. Finally, they reach the waters where they grew up.

We don't know how salmon can find their way on this long trip up the river. But we do know what they do when they get there.

With her tail and snout, the mother salmon digs a long hole at the bottom of the stream. She fills the hole with thousands of tiny eggs—eggs that will hatch into little salmon. She covers the eggs with sand and gravel to hide them and keep them safe.

The eggs hatch, and the baby salmon grow. When they are about as long as your finger, they are big enough to start the dangerous swim to the ocean. They float *backward* down the long river—tails first and heads last! They seem to steer better that way. On and on they drift and tumble.

Many of them never reach the ocean. Too many enemies—birds, animals, and bigger fish—wait along the way. The salmon that do reach the ocean start growing longer and wider and bigger. Then one day, they, too, start the long, hard trip up the river to the quiet waters where they were hatched.

*You may read about other fish
if you look up* Sardines *or* Sharks *in this book.*

Sand Everywhere

Sand.

Sand everywhere.

Sand down your neck, and sand between your toes.

Sand at the seashore. You can see it along the beach in two directions as far as you can look.

Sand in the desert. There you can see sand in *four* directions as far as you can look.

There is sand at the bottoms of rivers, sand piled up in hills, or *dunes,* at the edge of lakes, sand in mountain valleys, and sand under the earth and on top of the earth almost anywhere.

It wasn't always there. Where did it come from?

Most things start small and grow big. But sand starts big and grows small, though *grow* isn't exactly the right word. Sand doesn't *grow* small. It becomes that way when bigger things, mostly rocks, break into smaller pieces.

The wind, the frost, and the rain are great sand-makers. They work against high mountain cliffs . . . and slowly . . . slowly . . . through millions of years . . . they break off pieces of rock, which tumble down the mountainside. As the rock bangs and bounces, it breaks off other pieces of rock, at the same time breaking itself into smaller pieces. It isn't sand yet, but it's starting to be.

Rivers help make sand, too. The water of a river rushes down the mountainside, rolling rocks along and breaking them into smaller and smaller pieces. Glaciers are another good sand-maker. The heavy ice scrapes and grinds the rocks that it moves across. The ice also carries along the sand it has made and dumps it in places far away.

Another great sand-maker is the ocean. All over the world the tides rise and fall, and storm waves tear at the rocks along the shore, banging them together, wearing them down . . . until finally some of the rocks are so small that they are what we call *sand*.

Most brown sand comes from a hard mineral called *quartz*, mixed with broken rocks. White sand comes from coral and seashells that have been broken up by the wind and water. Lava, which flows from volcanoes, is often broken up into black sand. There are also red, gray, and green sands. There is even golden sand—specks of real gold—which sometimes collects at the bottoms of fast-moving streams.

You may read about Deserts *in Volume 4.*
"The Jewels That Mountains Wear"
under Ice *in Volume 8*
will tell you about glaciers.

Where Am I?

I am in an up-and-down city, built on many hills. Riding on its steep streets is like riding down the tallest hill of a roller coaster. At the top of a hill you look almost straight down and hope the brakes will hold.

On some streets little cars are pulled up and down the tracks

12

by long metal ropes, or *cables*. The tiny cars look like mechanical toys. *Clang! Clang! Clang!* go their warning bells. The cable cars are almost always crowded with passengers. Many of them are visitors to the city—*tourists*.

This city built beside a beautiful bay has fine weather—not too hot in summer, and warm enough the rest of the time so that flowers grow all winter. There is always the smell of the sea here.

Two great bridges reach across the bay, and another bridge is not far away. One of these bridges, painted a bright orange red, is famous all over the world. It's called the Golden Gate Bridge.

In the early days this city was just a tiny Spanish village. And then gold was discovered nearby. Hundreds of ships began sailing into the harbor as men came to hunt for gold.

The village grew and grew until there were huge warehouses, wharves, tall buildings, and fine homes. Maybe you have guessed its name. San Francisco! On the coast of California. It is one of the world's great cities. Even if you see it through fog, it's still beautiful. The fog comes in over and under the Golden Gate Bridge. It wisps through the tops of the eucalyptus trees and nudges the tops of tall buildings.

Look under Where Am I? *in Volume 16
and find San Francisco on the map.*

13

SARDINES

How the Sardines Get into the Cans

Wynken, Blynken, and Nod one night
    Sailed off in a wooden shoe—
Sailed on a river of crystal light
    Into a sea of dew.
"Where are you going, and what do you wish?"
    The old moon asked the three.
"We have come to fish for the herring fish
    That live in this beautiful sea;
Nets of silver and gold have we!"
    Said Wynken, Blynken, and Nod.

Sardines are really little fish called *herring*. In many places along the ocean shore, fishermen wait to hear the news by telephone or radio:

"The herring are here! The herring are here!"

Factory and can-company workers wait to hear the factory whistles "blowing for fish." They know they'll have work tomorrow.

The herring fish arrive in enormous numbers—millions and millions. Where do they come from? Nobody knows for sure. From out in the ocean somewhere. The slim, silvery-blue fish swim toward the land to find food. One of the things they like best is a tiny shrimp no bigger than your little finger. When fishermen see a lot of these shrimp in the water, they look for a lot of herring to follow.

For years and years and years, fishermen have watched for herring in the same way. A man sits in a little house built on a high place at the edge of the ocean. He stays there all night and all day, watching and listening.

From high in the air the sea gulls see the herring first. In the evening the fisherman listens for the excited screaming of the sea gulls to tell him the herring are here. In the daytime he can see the gulls circle and dive.

With its long, strong beak a gull picks a herring out of the water and flies away with it. (That is one sardine that will never get into a can!)

There's another way that the fishermen know when the herring have arrived. Herring are very oily fish. When many herring swim close together, oil comes to the top of the ocean and makes the water look slick. When fishermen see this oil slick, they know the herring are there.

Now they have to catch them.

The fishermen have a fish trap all ready and waiting. The fish trap, called a *weir,* is so big that it can hold a hundred barrels of herring. The fishermen make the trap from slim trees—birch trees when they can find them—that they have cut down in the woods. They drive the posts made from these trees into the bottom of the ocean and let them stick up above the water. Then they fasten a *seine,* or net, to the posts. Now they are ready to catch herring.

Looking for shrimp, the herring swim along the shore. They come to a brush fence the fishermen have built in the water. They swim along the fence, trying to find a way around it. The fence leads them into the big fish trap.

The trap is so big that a "sardine" boat can go inside it. A thick hose is put into the water. The fish are sucked into the boat the way dust is sucked into a vacuum-cleaner bag. When the boat first goes into the trap, it is empty and floating high on the water. When it is loaded with herring, it sinks so low under its weight of fish that the water sometimes splashes over the deck. Like most fish, sardines do not live long once they are taken out of the water.

The boat takes the fish to the sardine canning factory. The fish are pumped through a hose out of the boat and into the factory.

The whistle blows to let the people know that there are fish to put into cans. The people come. They sort the fish and fit them into the cans. They add oil or mustard or spices. A machine closes the cans, and the fish are cooked. The cans are then packed into boxes and taken by trucks and trains and boats to food stores all over the world.

And that is how sardines get into cans, ready for you to eat.

You may read about Factories *in Volume 6.*
And if you liked this story,
you'll like Salmon—*also in this book.*

Benjamin Barnes Goes to School

Benjamin Barnes crawled out from under the soft blue quilt. Something was different. Benjamin looked around his room.

"Nothing *looks* different," he thought to himself. He wiggled his toes on the cold floor. Then he saw the blue jeans and shirt folded neatly over his chair and the toes of his new sneakers sticking out from under the bed.

"School," he said softly. "Today I go to school! Mom—Mom!" he called in his loudest five-year-old voice.

Mrs. Barnes was already in the kitchen fixing breakfast.

"Benjamin," she answered, "time to get dressed. You don't want to be late on the first day of school!"

Benjamin was excited. His stomach felt so funny that he could hardly eat his cereal. And when it was time to walk the four long blocks to school, he held his mother's hand as tightly as he could.

When they were almost there, and Benjamin could see the wide front door of the school building, he looked at his mother and asked, "Will you stay with me?"

"I'll take you to your room, Ben, but you know that mothers aren't allowed to stay at school."

She gave his hand a tender squeeze and smiled. This made Benjamin feel a little better, but not much.

Mrs. Alter, Ben's teacher, stood smiling in the hall outside the kindergarten room. There were lots of children clattering toward the door. Some were laughing and talking as they hung up their coats and skipped past Mrs. Alter into the room. Some just looked inside, then up at their mothers.

Benjamin stared at the floor. He didn't move.

"Good morning. I'm Mrs. Alter," the teacher said, giving each child a special hello and smile.

"I don't want to go in there," he whispered to his mother.

"Your coat hook is over here, Benjamin. You won't have any trouble remembering where it is, because your name is pasted right above the hook."

It was a friendly grown-up voice. But it wasn't his mother's voice. Benjamin looked up, just a little. Out of the corner of his eye he saw Mrs. Alter. He raised his head a little more. BEN. It was his name! Ben's father had taught him how to make the letters.

"I'll be here when school is over, Ben," his mother said. "Then we'll go home to have lunch."

A big tear rolled down Ben's cheek.

"Do I *have* to stay?" said another boy's voice.

Ben turned around, forgetting for a minute his mother and home. There stood another boy, just about Ben's size. He clutched his mother's hand, too.

Mrs. Alter led both boys into the room as their mothers left. "Let's see what we can find for you and Arthur to do," she said.

Slowly Ben put one foot in front of the other. He blinked hard to keep the tears back. Most of the children were exploring the bright, sunny room—some quietly, others jumping up and down and giggling with excitement.

"Oooh! New crayons!"

"And puzzles!"

"What kind of animal is this? Is it a mouse?" a girl named Mary asked.

Mrs. Alter stopped in front of a large glass cage. "It's Amos, our hamster. He looks a little like a mouse. But he's bigger. And he gets very hungry. You can take turns feeding him when you come to school. Would you like to give Amos some food, Ben?"

Ben hung his head shyly. Amos looked soft and furry, just right for petting. But Ben thought only, "I want to go home."

"I would, Mrs. Alter," Mary said.

Several of the children watched as Mary took a piece of crisp lettuce from a bag next to the cage and dropped it inside.

There were big, shiny blocks. A box of dress-up clothes already had been emptied onto the floor.

There were dolls and a doll bed. A record player stood on a shelf with a stack of records next to it. Ben had a record player, too. He wondered if Mrs. Alter had some of the songs he liked to hear. But he was afraid to ask.

After a few minutes, Mrs. Alter played a soft chord on the piano. "Whenever you hear me play that chord," she said, "you'll know it's time to sit on the red rug."

A thick red rug was spread in the middle of the room. Mrs. Alter sat on a low chair at the edge. Ben and Arthur sat down next to each other.

Mrs. Alter smiled. "Now that you've had a chance to look around, I think we should learn names. I know a rhyme that will help:

> *Good morning to you.*
> *Good morning to you.*
> *My name is Mrs. Alter.*
> *How do you do?*

Only you say your own names instead. Who would like to begin?"

Several hands flew up. Ben smiled for the first time.

"I know that poem," he said in a small voice. "I heard it on my record at home."

"Well, then," Mrs. Alter said, "suppose you start, Ben."

Ben's stomach felt better. He stood up and said all the words. He didn't say them very loud at first, but at the last, he did.

"Will you be my friend?" a voice whispered when Ben had finished. It was Arthur.

After everyone was introduced, Mrs. Alter served juice and crackers and read a story from a book. Then she took the children to the playground. And what a playground! It had swings and a slide and a huge sandbox. Ben and Arthur tried them all.

The time had gone so quickly, everyone was surprised when Mrs. Alter said it was time to go home . . . and Ben looked up to see his mother.

"Here I am, Mom," Ben called over the chattering voices. "C'mon, Arthur. . . .This is my new friend, Arthur," he explained to his mother. "He didn't want to stay at school. But now we're friends. And there's a hamster. His name is Amos. And we played on the playground. And, Mom, can we get here early tomorrow? I didn't have a turn at playing with the blocks."

Mrs. Barnes hugged her son. She smiled at Mrs. Alter. Mrs. Alter smiled and winked at Ben. He winked back. Benjamin Barnes's first day at school was over.

The Boy Who Looked Out the Window

Whenever Ralph's mother asked him, "What did you do in school today?" Ralph always answered, "Oh—nothing."

While the other boys and girls were reading and learning how to count, Ralph was looking out the window, thinking about playing outside. When Miss Duffy, his teacher, asked him a question, Ralph often didn't know the answer.

"I wasn't listening," Ralph would tell his teacher. "I was thinking about playing outside."

Miss Duffy didn't know what to do about Ralph. She tried everything she could think of, but nothing seemed to work. Then she got an idea. She talked to some of the other teachers about her idea.

The next morning Miss Duffy asked Ralph to take a note to Miss Travino's second grade class at the end of the hall.

The children in Miss Travino's classroom were reading.

"I'll be with you in a minute," Miss Travino told Ralph, "as soon as Susan finishes the page."

Everyone was looking at his book while Susan read: "Sally stops. She looks out the window. What does she see?"

"Good, Susie," said Miss Travino. She turned to read Ralph's note, and Ralph looked down at Susie's book.

He saw a picture of a girl. She was looking through a window at a man leading a strange animal on a leash. Next to the picture was some writing. Ralph wished he knew who the man was and why he was bringing the funny-looking animal to the girl's house.

Miss Travino thanked Ralph and said, "Take this note next door to the third grade, to Mrs. Jackus' room."

"Excuse me," Ralph said from the doorway. "I have a note from Miss Duffy."

"You'll have to wait just a minute," the teacher said, smiling, "we're in the middle of a problem."

She turned to her class. "If each of the three boys has 10 cents, do they have enough to buy the pint of ice cream?"

One girl raised her hand.

"Yes," she said.

Ralph wondered how she knew.

"How do you know?" asked Mrs. Jackus.

"Because it says a pint of ice cream costs 30 cents, and 3 times 10 is 30."

"Right," said Mrs. Jackus.

Mrs. Jackus read the note and sent Ralph to the fourth grade, next door. The window shades in that room were drawn. Ralph stood outside and peered into the dark room. The teacher was projecting colored slides on a screen.

"Just have a seat," the teacher said to Ralph. "We'll be through in a few minutes."

28

Ralph found a seat. The slide being projected showed a house on a boat floating in a river.

"This is a houseboat," said the teacher. "The Chinese call it a *sampan*. For many families this kind of boat is home."

Ralph wondered what it would be like to live on a sampan.

When the lights came on, the teacher told Ralph, "We're studying China right now, and Jerry's uncle sent him some slides."

Ralph wished he could hear more about the people who lived in houseboats, but the teacher looked at the note and sent him to the fifth grade.

The children in the fifth grade were gathered around a workbench. Ralph came into the room quietly and squeezed between two girls at the end of the bench. On the bench was a battery to make electricity.

Two wires, one on each side of the battery, went into a tank of water. The end of each wire was turned up and covered by a long, upside-down glass tube filled with water. Bubbles were appearing on the wires and rising to the top of each tube.

The teacher pointed to the tubes.

"Now you are beginning to see the oxygen and hydrogen bubbles forming," he said. Water is made of hydrogen and oxygen —two gases that don't seem anything like water."

"Now, I'll explain how the electricity does this," the teacher began. Then he noticed Ralph.

"Did you want something?" the teacher asked Ralph.

"I want to know how the electricity does it," Ralph said, and the class laughed.

Ralph suddenly remembered the note in his hand. He gave it to the teacher, who read it and sent him to the sixth grade.

In this grade Ralph found the children singing a bouncy song. It made Ralph smile as he stood in the doorway and listened.

When the song had ended, Ralph told the teacher, "I have a note."

"Sing it," said one of the boys. Everyone laughed.

"It's not *that* kind of note," the teacher said. She thanked

Ralph, read the note, and told him to go back to Miss Duffy's room.

Later, Ralph said to Miss Duffy, "I wish we could learn some of the things the bigger kids learn."

"You will," said Miss Duffy. "But first you have to learn some beginning things—like reading. You'll need the things you learn in the first grade to help you learn more in the second and all the other grades."

That evening, when his mother asked, "What did you do in school today?" Ralph had an answer.

"I started to get ready to learn all about everything," he said excitedly. "Music, figuring things out, Chinese people living on boats, how to take water apart—everything!"

If you liked this story,
you'll like Teachers *in Volume 15.*

A Very Famous Doctor

Once there was a little boy who loved all living things so much he did not want to see any animal or person hurt. One time he was with a friend who was going to use a slingshot to shoot at some birds sitting in a field. The boy ran out into the field and shooed the birds away before his friend could hit them. This boy grew up to be a very famous man. His name was Albert Schweitzer.

Albert Schweitzer first became famous as a writer and a musician. But then he asked himself what he could do to help people the most. He decided to study to be a doctor so that he could make sick people well and keep them from pain. In America and Europe there were many doctors. Africa was one place that had many sick people but few doctors. Dr. Schweitzer went to Africa to help these sick people get well.

The doctor took big boxes of medicine with him to Africa. He had to travel in a canoe on dangerous rivers through hot, green jungles. Huge snakes hung down from the limbs of trees. He could hear animals crashing through the forest and birds chattering.

At first the people of Africa were afraid of the new white doctor.

But soon they understood that he was their friend, and they helped him build his first little hospital on the bank of a river. Some sick people walked to his hospital, traveling on jungle trails. Others came in boats made from logs. Children with big sores all over their bodies were brought to the hospital. Some people came who had been bitten by snakes or by big spiders. Dr. Schweitzer worked all day every day, and many nights, helping these people. As time went on, other doctors and many nurses came to help him.

When he ran out of money and needed more medicine and hospital supplies, he would go all the way back to Europe to give lectures and play organ recitals. Then he would return to Africa. Later he built a bigger hospital. He spent most of his life in Africa, not only helping the sick but also teaching the people how to help each other.

If you liked this story, you may read about Africa *in Volume 1 and about* Medicine *in Volume 10.*

Water Clowns

These rocks at the edge of San Francisco's beach are known all over the world. People come from far away to see them. Or really to see the brown animals that live on them.

People say, "Oh, *there* they are! Listen to them barking!"

The animals do sound something like dogs. But they are fur-covered seals. Well . . . people *call* them seals, and these rocks are known everywhere as Seal Rocks, but the animals really are *sea lions*.

There are many other rocks along the coast where sea lions live, but these are the most famous ones.

You can tell the difference between seals and sea lions by their ears. True seals have no outside ears, just tiny holes to hear through. Sea lions have small outside ears.

Seals and sea lions have finned flippers instead of feet. They are land-and-water animals. Their food is mostly fish, squid, and shellfish, and they swallow it whole.

Swimming in the water, seals are swift and graceful. But on land they go flip-flopping along on their flippers with an awkward waddle.

Seals and sea lions sleep on land, and their babies, or *pups,* as they are called, are born on land. When it's time to learn to swim, a mother picks up her pup by the back of its neck, just as a mother cat picks up a kitten. Then she carries it to the water for its first swimming lesson. After a few weeks, a group of baby seals will go into the water and dive and play like children.

The trained seals in circuses and zoos are really the seals with outside ears—the California sea lions. They are very smart and love to play and are easily trained to do tricks. A sea lion can be taught to balance a big rubber ball on the end of its nose or play a tune on a row of trumpets. *You* might play the trumpets, but could you balance the ball?

Sea lions like the way people clap their hands after a trick. Sometimes sea lions even applaud themselves by clapping their front flippers together!

What sea lions like most of all is fish. So every time a sea lion does a trick, its trainer tosses it a piece of fish. The idea seems to be—do a trick, get a fish.

There are more seals in the cold, frozen Far North than in any other place. These are the fur seals, the true seals with no outside ears. Their coats are thick and beautiful, and underneath they have a layer of *blubber,* or fat, to keep them warm.

The small harbor seals live along reefs and coastal islands or in lakes. Though shy, they like company, and if you are friendly, they will be friendly, too.

Harbor seals make good pets, but maybe not house pets. Your father might not like one in his favorite chair! And what would your mother say if it flopped its muddy flippers over her clean rug?

Let's Go Out and Play

38

"Mother," Danny said, "Shep and I want to go outdoors and play in the snow."

"All right," Danny's mother said. "Put on your snowsuit and your boots and your scarf and your mittens."

"Oh, phooey! Why?"

"Because you'll be cold if you don't."

"Shep doesn't have to put on clothes to go outdoors. If a dog doesn't, why do I?"

"The dog doesn't get cold in the snow."

"Why doesn't he?"

"Because Shep adapts."

"He *what?*" Danny asked.

Danny's mother laughed. "In the summer Shep's hair is short and thin, and he stays cool. In the winter his hair gets longer and thicker and helps keep him warm. It's the same with horses, cows, and rabbits. Some animals grow whole new coats of hair to help keep them warm in winter. That's called *adapting* to the weather."

"Well, I wish I could adapt! It would be better than putting on all these old winter clothes."

"But wouldn't you look strange with long, thick hair all over you?"

"I guess so. But I'm still not going to put on all those heavy old clothes. I guess I'll stay inside and look at my picture books."

On the first few pages of his picture book Danny saw ants and birds and bears. In each picture the ants, the birds, and the bears were enjoying a nice summer day.

"What do *they* do when winter comes?" Danny asked his mother. "Do they adapt, too?"

"Indeed they do," his mother said.

"How do they?"

"Well, a bear adapts by eating all summer so that he gets very fat. The fat helps keep him warm in winter. He crawls into his den, snuggles cosily—and spends the winter asleep."

"All winter?"

"Most of it."

"I wouldn't want to sleep all winter. I'd rather be a boy and adapt by putting on a snowsuit. What about birds? Do they curl up in dens, too?"

"No. Some birds get thick winter feathers. But most of them just fly away to the South where it's warmer."

"Oh, well," Danny said. "I can't fly, and I can't grow feathers. I guess I'm stuck with my snowsuit—hey, wait a minute. What about ants? I never saw a *fat* ant. And *they* don't fly south do they?"

"No. Ants are something like bears. In winter they crawl into the ground."

"I know—and sleep practically all winter. That's not for me!" Danny turned to his dog and said, "Come on, Shep. It's still snowing. Let's go outside and play. I'll *adapt* by putting on my snowsuit and boots and scarf and mittens."

Want to know more?
Read "The Special Long Sleep" *under* Animals
in Volume 1. You may read about each season
if you look under Fall, Spring, Summer, *and* Winter.

41

Seeds That Fly

Puff!
He's blowing at a fluffy dandelion—and soon hundreds of new
dandelion plants may begin to grow.

It's fun to blow at a dandelion
and watch the seeds fly.

Usually a gust of wind sweeps
the dandelion seeds off the plant
and into the air. Low and high,
they dip and fly until they drop
softly to the ground.

If a seed lands in a place that's
good for growing, and if there's
just the right amount of rain and
sunshine needed for that kind of
seed, then one day it may
become a new dandelion plant.

A *seed* is the part of a plant
from which a new plant grows.
The seed can be as small as a
speck of dust or as big as a
coconut.

Inside each dandelion seed is a tiny plant and a bit of plant food.

And on the outside there's a covering called a *seed coat*. The seed coat protects everything that's inside.

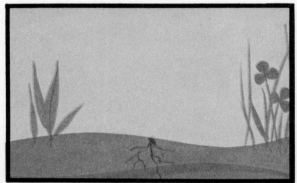

When the seed starts to grow, a tiny point pushes down into the ground. That's the *root*.

Then another little shoot pushes up into the air. That's the *stem*.

Dandelion seeds are not the only seeds that fly with the breezes.

The two-winged seeds of a maple tree spin and twirl to the ground like toy propellers.

From just one maple tree, thousands and thousands of seeds will fall and whirl.

Many of the seeds that fall do not grow into plants. Animals eat many of them. Bears, beavers, chipmunks, and squirrels feast on them. Hungry little mice and big rats, too, devour seeds. Birds gobble them up.

Many seeds land in places where they can't grow.

Some seeds float on water.

Other seeds are caught in animal fur and may be carried for miles.

Pine seeds drop from pine cones and glide through the air. They fall to the ground slowly, on just one wing.

The spurting cucumber *pops* its seeds into the air.

Want to learn more?
Read Helicopters *in Volume 7.*

Who Wrote That Play?

"Banish the fools!"

"Zounds! What rogues and rascals they!"

"Madmen! Be off with them!"

"Didst ever thou see or hear a play so foul?"

The people shouting these strange words long ago in England were part of the audience at the Globe Theater in London. They didn't like the play, and they were not afraid to say so.

They probably had arrived at the theater many hours before the play started—to be sure they would find a good place to stand. Only the very rich could afford seats. The other people stood on the ground. (They were called *groundlings*.)

There was no roof on the theater. The ground was dusty when the weather was dry, and muddy when it rained. People shivered from the cold and fog. The only light other than that from torches on the stage came from the sky.

When the people in the audience were pleased, they cheered and clapped. But when they were bored or disagreed with what the actors said, they booed . . . they yelled . . . they shouted. They threw food at the stage. Sometimes they even jumped onto the stage to complain. Any play performed at the Globe had to be really good to make the audience listen.

Women weren't allowed to play parts. So the men actors had to pretend to be women, children, even animals!

Probably no one guessed that one of the young men who wrote plays for the Globe Theater would turn out to be one of the greatest known writers. His name was William Shakespeare, and he was born more than 400 years ago.

We don't know very much about Shakespeare as a child. But we do know that he traveled to London from his home in Stratford-upon-Avon, England, when he was still a young man. In London, Shakespeare saw people on crowded, dirty streets. He met thieves and soldiers and people of royal families. He read about kings and queens.

He acted in plays written by others. And he wrote his own. Shakespeare wrote happy plays and also sad plays and plays about great battles. He even made up words that are still used today—words like *gloomy* and *hurry*.

In Shakespeare's plays, the *characters*, or people that the actors pretended to be, were like the people he had met and read about. In those days many believed in ghosts and witches. So Shakespeare made them characters, too. And because audiences loved poetry and music, he filled his plays with verses and songs.

Today our theaters don't look like the Globe. People who come to watch a play sit in seats. They are quieter, and they don't jump onto the stage to shout at the actors.

But Shakespeare's plays are so good that it doesn't matter where they are performed or when they were written. People everywhere still go to see them.

The Shapes of Things

All the shapes of the blocks you use for building things at home or at school can be seen downtown.

Hold someone's hand as you stand downtown on the sidewalk. Close your eyes. Tight . . . tighter. Now open them halfway. Take a long look all around through your half-closed eyes. What do you see?

Shapes. All kinds of shapes.

The long thin shapes of skyscrapers reaching high.

50

The square shapes of buildings not so high.

The shapes of windows, long or square, everywhere.

The round shapes of tires on automobiles, buses, and trucks.

Now open your eyes wide. The city buildings are still here, all about you, but some of the shapes are gone—no, not really gone. You just don't notice them so much now.

Or do you?

Danger! Sharks!

This man is taking photographs of the beautiful, bright-colored fish that live in the ocean. Suddenly, he sees a giant shape. It looks at first like a long, dark shadow.

The man doesn't wait to see any more because he knows that this big shadow thing is really a shark. And some sharks eat people!

Because some sharks are dangerous, a wire net is stretched along the shore, out in the water, at beaches where sharks have been seen. This keeps the sharks away and makes it safe to swim there. Many large beaches have been made safe for swimming.

Sharks aren't everywhere in the ocean, and not all sharks are man-eaters. But these great white sharks are. They are so fierce that fishermen call them tigers of the sea.

It's hard for a man to fight them because they are such strong, fast swimmers and have bodies that are protected by a tough skin covered with tiny, toothlike bones. In their big mouths are rows and rows of sharp teeth that rip like the edge of a saw. White sharks make a quick meal out of almost anything!

This is another man-eating shark. You may think he looks too funny to be dangerous, but he's really too dangerous to be funny.

He's called the hammerhead shark. If you hold the book sideways, you can see why.

These small dogfish sharks can bite, but they are not likely to eat people. They are a big pest to a fisherman. The fish they don't eat, they scare away. Sometimes they even eat the fisherman's net.

It's only because they have faces that look a little like a dog's that they are named after man's friendliest pet.

The whale shark is a whale of a shark—the largest shark of all. But in spite of its size, it is one of the most harmless—unless you're a small fish. It eats small fish and doesn't attack large fish or people.

Some men work at catching sharks. They go hunting for them nearly every day. It is the way they make their money.

Just about every part of this big, dangerous fish is good for something.

The oil in a shark's liver contains vitamin A.

The skin of a shark makes a very tough leather
for belts and other things.

Some people collect shark teeth. You can find them in the sand on
many ocean shores. You can even make them into a necklace.

The meat of a shark is good to eat. But there are more sharks
caught than people want to eat, so some shark meat is made into
fertilizer. Farmers put fertilizer on their land to help things grow.

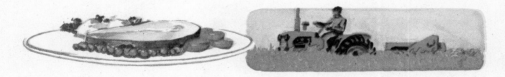

Even the fins of a shark are good for something. People in China
use them to make a soup.

Are you interested in underwater life? Read Aquanauts *in Volume 1
or any of the articles under* Ocean *in Volume 11.*

Follow the Leader

Mary had a little lamb,
Its fleece was white as snow.
And everywhere that Mary went,
The lamb was sure to go!

This is a very old nursery rhyme. And it tells some facts about lambs—and sheep.

Most lambs and sheep (which are grown-up lambs) are really *almost* as white as snow. They are when they are clean. But lambs, like boys and girls, get dirty!

Of course, not all sheep are white. Remember *"Baa, baa, Black Sheep, have you any wool?"* And there are some brown sheep, too.

Like Mary's little lamb, sheep like to follow. They follow one another quite readily. This makes it easy for the man who takes care of the sheep. If the man—called a *shepherd*—can get one or two sheep going in the right direction, the rest will follow right along.

Sometimes a shepherd has dogs to help him keep the sheep from getting lost.

But there's a lot more to sheep than is told in "Mary Had a Little Lamb." Sheep give milk that makes good cheese.

Sheep are covered with long, thick, soft hair called *wool*. Some clothes and blankets are made from wool.

59

To get wool from the sheep, men must cut it off—much like barbers giving haircuts. The sheep are lucky, though—they get haircuts only once a year, at a time when they won't be too cold without their wool. Afterward, they look rather thin and strange, but they feel all right.

Sheep do something else that people do. They have to take baths. They are herded into tanks of water called *sheep-dips*. Medicine is put into the water to protect the sheep from sickness. And sheep have to have shots from a sheep doctor, too! Only they don't say "ouch!" They say, "*Baaaaa-aaaaaa!*"

In sheep's wool there is a grease called *lanolin*. Lanolin is used in skin creams to help make your hands soft and smooth again when they have become chapped from the cold.

Just about anyplace you find people, you will find sheep—
except in cities, of course.

Although sheep are gentle, mild animals, they are also tough.
They can live in high, cold, rocky country and in places that are
almost deserts.

Wherever they live, sheep look pretty much alike. However,
there is one kind of sheep that grows a tail so long and heavy that
the shepherd has to make a little cart to put under its tail to keep
it from dragging on the ground.

These certainly could not be the same kind of sheep that
belonged to Bo-Peep! Remember?

> *Little Bo-Peep has lost her sheep,*
> *And can't tell where to find them.*
> *Leave them alone, and they'll come home,*
> *Wagging their tails behind them!*

Animals That Live in Shells

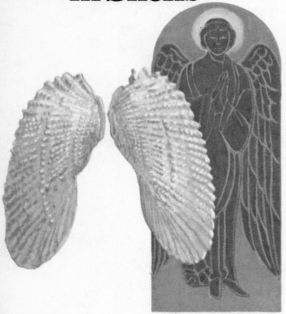

Angel wings

Moon shell

Top shell

There are many different shelled animals. The smallest live in shells as tiny as the letter *o*. The largest are found in the ocean near Australia and weigh nearly 600 pounds!

There have been times when a pearl diver has accidentally put his arm into the open shell of a giant clam. The clam tried to close its shell, to protect itself, and caught the diver. Because of accidents like that, this giant shelled animal is sometimes called the *man-eating clam*.

Some shells are all in one piece. They are called *univalves*. Other shells are made up of two pieces that are the same size and fit together perfectly. A hinge holds the two-piece shell together. These shells are called *bivalves*.

What do these shells look like to you?

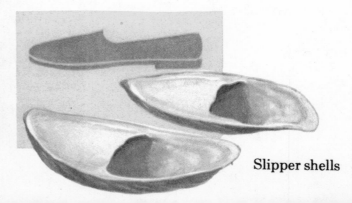

Slipper shells

Shells are really one-room houses. Each shell has room for just one kind of animal. Scientists call the little animals *mollusks*.

Although most mollusks live in the water, some are found on land. This snail lives in the forest and lays its eggs in the ground. In the picture the eggs have been very much enlarged so that you can see them, for they are very tiny.

When they are born, mollusks do not have backbones like other animals. Most of them have very little bony stuff. They are soft and squishy and helpless. Mollusks need protection from enemies that would eat them. They get this protection from the shell they build around themselves. Mollusks can build a house out of their own bodies.

Of course, baby mollusks do not really *build* houses. They *grow* houses. (It is as easy for them to do this as it is for you to grow fingernails.)

Mollusks eat the tiny bits of food that float with the moving seawater. Part of their food is used to build their bodies. The other part is used to build their shells. Mollusks are covered with a kind of thin second skin called a *mantle*. The part of the food that is used to build the shell oozes out on top of the mantle and hardens.

Finally, the mantle is covered by a hard shell. Now the mollusks have protection. A mollusk and its shell will keep on growing as long as the mollusk lives. They have been known to live in their shells and continue adding on to them for as long as 20 years. By then the shell has gotten quite large.

The smaller shell is one year old, about average for this kind of mollusk. The larger shell was lived in and built on to for 20 years.

Most of the time, the shells that we find are empty. The mollusks that lived in them have been eaten by fish or birds, or they have simply died and dried up in the hot sun. But sometimes, especially after a big storm at sea, you will find a mollusk at home. The waves will have lifted the mollusk, shell and all, up onto the beach.

Some of us have a way of calling *all* shells seashells. But all shells are not found in the sea. You can find shells on riverbanks and on lakefronts. You can find shells at the edge of ponds and streams. There are shells to be found in rain forests, and you may even find them in your backyard.

Did this story interest you?
Then read Coral *in Volume 3*
and Oysters *in Volume 11.*

Traveling on Water

The very first boat in the world . . .
What was it? A log?

That's a pretty good guess. A man could sit on a log and go floating down a river. If he paddled with his hands, he could make the log go a tiny, tiny bit faster. He could even turn it slowly.

But a log can flop and make you go plop. *Splash!* You're dripping wet.

Maybe one day someone tied three or four logs together with vines. This made something called a *raft*. A raft doesn't tip easily — but it moves no faster than a log, and it is hard to steer.

One day someone tried making a hollow place in a log where he could sit and where he could carry things. It seemed like a good idea, and other people started making these log boats. Sometimes the hollow place in the log was burned out with fire. Sometimes it was dug out with sharp sticks and stones.

People stopped using their hands for paddles. They used a flat stick instead. This made their log boat go faster.

Nobody knows who was first to put a sail on a boat. Maybe it was someone who saw a leaf being blown along on top of the water. We don't know what was used for the first sail. Maybe wide, tough leaves or woven grass. Maybe wide pieces of bark or bamboo. Whatever it was, people found that sailing was faster and easier than paddling.

Finally, someone built a ship that used a sail *and* long paddles, called *oars*. When there was no wind, the sailors rowed with the oars. When the wind blew in the same direction they were going, they put up the sail. Later, sailors learned to turn, or *set*, a sail to make the boat go in almost any direction they wished.

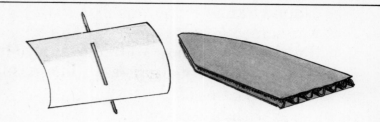

To see how the wind pushes a sailboat, make a sail out of a small piece of stiff paper and put a toothpick through it. Then push the toothpick into a cork or a piece of cardboard or a piece of bubbly foam plastic. Put it in a pan of water and blow on it. Pretend that your boat is sailing across the ocean.

When you stop blowing, what happens to your boat?

It stops, too. A sailboat goes only when the wind blows.

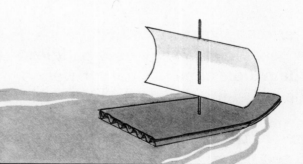

This big boat, with a sail and oars, was built long ago in the country of Greece.

People learned how to build sailing ships with masts so high they seemed to touch the sky. These ships had so many sails that oars were not needed.

After many years of sailing, people found a still better way to make boats move. They used paddles again, but this time they put the paddles in a wheel that was part of the boat. When the paddle wheel moved, the boat moved whether the wind blew or not.

Some of the paddle wheels were as big as a house! They were much too heavy to turn by hand. People had to use something new to make the paddle wheel turn.

They used steam. Steam turned an engine, and the engine turned the paddle wheel. Steamboats, with their tall chimneys puffing smoke and their steam whistles going *toot-toot,* sailed up and down the rivers and across lakes and oceans all over the world.

Today, there are many more kinds of engines that can make boats move. There are huge, fast ships with engines somewhat like those used in the big trucks that go roaring over the highways. Some boat engines even run with atomic power.

But all of the old kinds of boats are still used, too—sailboats, rowboats, canoes, and rafts.

Not very many people ride on a log anymore. But you still can if you want to.

If you liked this story, you'll like Rafts *in Volume 13. And read about* Mark Twain *(Volume 15), who spent much time on Mississippi River steamboats.*

How Did the Ship Get into the Bottle?

If you were a sailor on a ship, what would you do when you weren't working? Except when there's a storm, a sailor doesn't have to work all the time.

So what would you do? You could read or sleep. You could talk with your friends—if *they* weren't working. Or you could walk around the deck and look at the sky and ocean. But on a long, long trip you would probably get tired of these things.

Many sailors spend their spare time cutting, or *whittling,* things out of wood. Some sailors patiently carve small models of big things.

A sailor made this model of a ship and put it in the bottle.

Some people think that after the ship was made, it was taken to a bottle factory and that a bottle was made around the ship.

What do *you* think?

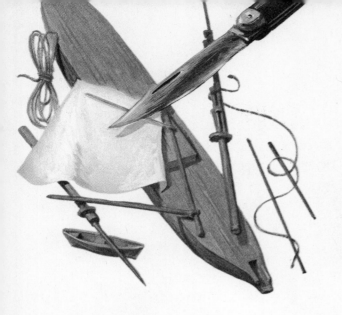

First, the sailor whittled out all the different parts of the ship. Then, carefully, he fitted each part to the next one.

He cut the sails out of cloth and fastened them to the big masts, and to the little masts, called *spars*.

Then he *rigged* the ship—fastened strings between all the masts and spars and sails to hold them in their proper places.

The masts and spars were too big to go into the bottle any way except endways. So he placed the masts right next to their holes and let them lie back flat on the ship's deck.

Then, so-o-o-o carefully, he slid everything endways into the bottle.

73

Now we're ready for the big trick.

Before the sailor slid the ship into the bottle, he tied a special long string to the masts and let the end of the string hang out.

With the ship snugly inside the bottle, he pulled the string and —presto—up came the masts and sails.

After the sailor cut the string off, there was no way to tell how the boat got into the bottle. It looked as if it had always been there.

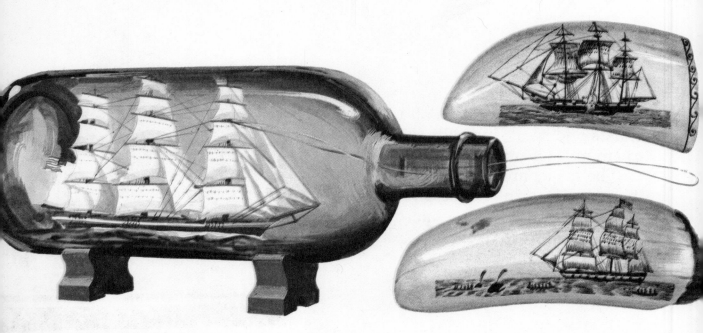

Sailors also used to carve pictures in their spare time. Here is one carved on a piece of ivory. Usually, the ivory came from the long, curved tooth of a walrus, called a *tusk*. Sometimes it came from an elephant's tusk. Sailors also carved pictures on shells and whales' teeth. These carvings were called *scrimshaw*. Why? Nobody knows. Maybe a sailor named Scrimshaw carved especially good ones.

The oldest carvings of ship models that we know about were made by the Egyptians—the same people who made the great stone pyramids. This is the model of an Egyptian ship carved from wood.

Far south in the ocean there are beautiful islands where palm trees and shining green plants grow. In the sun and the rain the plants grow fast and big. The people in these South Sea islands make toy boats for their children from the nuts and seeds dropped by these giant plants.

You can make models, too. You can make them out of almost anything—even folded pieces of paper. But it will take a lot of practice before you can make a big ship and put it inside a little bottle.

Would you like to learn about other hobbies? Read Hobbies *in Volume 7 or look under* Rocks *in Volume 13 and learn about "rock hounds."*

The Battle of the Iron Ships

Shug-chug-chug-chug. Shug-chug-chug-chug. The battleship *Monitor* is steaming straight for the battleship *Virginia*. The sailors are shoving a shell into the *Monitor's* forward cannon. *Clank!* They've locked the gun and . . . *varoom!* A puff of smoke. *Splash!* The shell hits the water. It misses its target.

The cannon keeps shooting.

People watching from the shore hold their hands over their ears, waiting for each blast. When it comes, some of the ladies scream.

Bavoom! Bavoom! Bavoom! Small children sitting on their father's shoulders squeal at each boom and flash.

Finally a shell from the *Monitor's* cannon hits the *Virginia*. But wait a minute—it bounces off the iron side without making a hole!

"Yay!" The men on the *Virginia* are cheering. Now the wooden battleship *Minnesota* moves in, firing its guns at the *Virginia*. Oh! The ironclad *Virginia* is turning its guns on the *Minnesota*.

Boom! Va-room! The wooden ship may not be so lucky. *Crash!* The *Minnesota's* on fire!

The flames are crawling up the *Minnesota's* mast. You can see them reflected in the water. It looks as if the water is on fire. . . .

Boom-bavoom! Boom! Boom! The battle has been going on for hours. *Splash! Splash! Boom-boom-boom!*

The *Monitor* and the *Virginia* pound each other with their cannon shells. Sometimes they are half a mile apart—sometimes they are nearly close enough to touch. *Boom-gadoom-aroom!* Neither ship can sink the other. The *Virginia* is the first to stop the fighting and steam away.

It was more than 100 years ago, on March 9, 1862—the day when the first iron ships that were ever built fought this famous battle.

The battle between the *Virginia* and the *Monitor* happened during the American Civil War. (The *Virginia* was once called the *Merrimack,* but this was before it was made into an iron ship.)

After that historic fight, most of the battleships that were built anywhere in the world were made of iron or steel—not wood—because this battle proved that metal ships could not easily be sunk, even with big guns!

More About Ships

Ships that can move along under the water, as well as on top of the water, are called *submarines*.

The very first submarines were quite different from the nuclear-powered subs of today—sometimes called *nukes*. Some of the early subs had greased leather sides, oars for rowing, wheels for traveling on the bottom, sails for moving on the surface, and long tubes that stuck out of the water to bring air to the submarine below.

The three main problems with all submarines are: how to make the sub sink and then come back up; how to steer the sub; and how to keep it filled with clean, fresh air when it is under the water.

Different ways have been tried for making a sub sink and rise. The one way that is still used is to build a sub with a double wall. The space between the walls can be filled with water when the captain wants to go down. The water makes the sub heavier, and it sinks, or *submerges*.

When it is time to come to the surface again, the water is forced out from between the walls. This makes the sub lighter, and it comes up, or *surfaces*.

For many years, problems kept the submarine from being very useful.

After it submerged, the sub had to use its air very carefully, and even then the air didn't last very long. Also, the batteries that supplied electric power

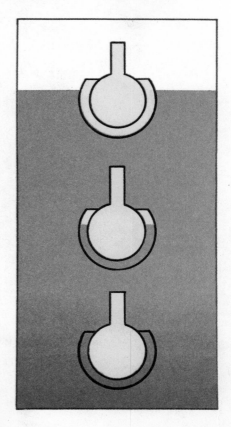

80

underwater used up their power very quickly and needed to be recharged. Before it ran out of either air or electric power, the sub had to surface.

Another reason the early subs were always surfacing was to see where they were going.

Inventors finally found ways for telling directions underwater, but the really big change in submarines came when the first nuclear subs were built.

The *nuclear reactor*—where the energy comes from—supplies almost unlimited power. This power runs the sub. And it runs generators that make electricity for the sub and that take oxygen out of the seawater for the sailors to breathe. The same generators can also run the sub's air conditioners.

The air conditioners keep the sub's air more pure than the air that sailors breathe when they leave the sub. So a nuclear sub can stay submerged for many, many days. The nuke *Triton* submerged . . . and went underwater all the way around the world! It took 84 days, and yet it did not surface once until the trip was over.

Nukes have sailed under the ice cap at the North Pole. The crew from the nuke *Seadragon* climbed onto the ice at the North Pole and played baseball.

A nuclear sub may not be like home, but sailors on today's submarines have movies, libraries, freshwater showers, exercise rooms, and excellent food.

Want to know more? Look up Future *in Volume 6 and* Jules Verne *in Volume 16.*

Smoke Signals

This traffic light is a signal. It says something quickly and clearly to you.

It tells you when you may cross the street safely and when you must wait for cars to go by.

This smoke is a signal, too. It was a signal used by the American Indians long ago. To make their signal, the Indians first

gathered up a pile of sticks and wood and set it on fire. They usually used damp wood because it burned more slowly and made a heavier smoke. After the wood was smoking, they held a blanket or large animal skin over the smoking wood. If they pulled the blanket off quickly, they could make a small puff of smoke. If they held the blanket down a longer time, they could make a large black puff of smoke.

82

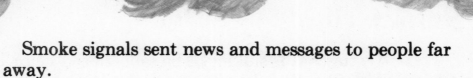

Smoke signals sent news and messages to people far away.

The signals meant different things to different Indian tribes. To one tribe these six puffs of smoke might mean, "Come on, the hunting is good here." To another tribe it might mean, "Help! Our enemies are coming!"

At night, when it was too dark to see smoke, the Indians made big bonfires on high ground. Then they used fire instead of smoke to make their signals.

Sometimes they made fire signals with burning arrows. When the flaming arrows told good news, the rest of the tribe must have been happy to see them.

Other kinds of signals are called landmarks.
Read about them under Directions *in Volume 4.*

SOS

This little tugboat is sinking! The sailors need help. They need it fast. Who will rescue them?

Far in the distance, the sailors can see another ship. That other ship could save them. It's a big ocean liner, with lifeboats, rafts, a doctor, and nurses.

The sailors shout for help. But the other ship is too far away. Nobody can hear their shouts.

The sailors wave their arms. But nobody on the other ship sees them.

What can the sailors do now?

There are several things they can do.

They can signal for help with light.

They can shoot up something like a skyrocket, a flare that will make a bright light high in the sky. If a sailor on that other ship sees the sudden, bright light, he will know that help is needed. The signal will be answered. The big ship will come to the rescue of the sinking tugboat.

They can signal for help with a searchlight. The searchlight makes a long bright path of light in the sky. It is like a long finger pointing, and it can be seen many miles away.

One sailor flicks the light on, then off . . . on, then off. . . . *He's spelling out a message in light.* Three short flashes of light spell the letter *S*. Three longer flashes of light spell *O*. And another three short flashes spell *S*.

SOS is the signal for *Help!* When a sailor on that other ship sees the flashing searchlight, the rescue can begin.

In the daylight the sailor can use a special mirror that catches sunlight and sends his message. The flashing light can be used in the daytime, as a searchlight is used at night.

They can signal with sound.

Even when a sailor's shouts can't be heard, other sounds travel across the water. Sharp blasts of the ship's powerful horn will let any nearby vessel know that help is needed.

The radioman can also speak into his microphone. "Mayday," he says. "Mayday, Mayday!" That's a signal word to let any-one know that help is needed. The message will be heard on the radios of any nearby ships or airplanes.

But what if rescuers are on the way, and they need to be told something important?

A sailor can use flags to signal the sailors on the liner that a doctor and a nurse and warm, dry blankets are needed.

If you liked this story, you'll like Lighthouses *in Volume 9.*

The Legless Wonders

It squirms, it wriggles.
It can glide and shake.
It's a legless wonder—
It's a *snake!*

You might think that this green garden snake is about to get tangled up in its own tail. But it isn't. Wriggling and slithering, this snake goes exactly where it wants to go.

Fish use their fins and tails to wriggle through water. And snakes certainly have tails. Except for its head, you could say that the rest of a snake *is* a tail. At least, it looks that way. But snakes don't have fins. They don't have legs.

Then how do they move?

Snakes have scales. They wouldn't be able to move much without them. Their long bodies loop, and the scales push against the ground. Twisting and turning, snakes gracefully glide along, over rocks and logs, and even through mud and sand.

Snakes *look* slippery and slimy. But they're not. Their skin actually feels like cool, soft leather.

Here's another thing about a snake's skin—it comes off!

When *you* grow, your skin grows, too. But not a snake's. As a snake gets bigger, its skin gets tighter and tighter until the snake wiggles right out of it—wearing a new skin that it has grown. The old skin turns inside out as the snake crawls out of it, so that it looks like the old skin has come off backwards. A snake sheds its skin a few times a year.

Most snakes won't hurt you if you leave them alone. Even some of the most dangerous of these long, twisting reptiles are so afraid of people that they will wriggle away as fast as they can if they see you first.

Snakes can't travel very far in cold weather. Their bodies become too stiff to move. So if you see any snakes taking an early morning sunbath on a rock, they're probably trying to get warm. After the snakes are warm enough, they will slither away and crawl under a shady rock or log.

In places where the winter is cold, snakes hide between rocks or under the ground. They sleep their long, special sleep called *hibernation*.

In some kinds of snakes the eggs hatch inside the mother snake's body. In other kinds the eggs hatch outside in a nest the snake makes for them in leaves or rotten wood or warm sand. When the babies are born, they wriggle and crawl away to find their own food.

Some snakes are as small as worms. Some are so large they can swallow a goat or a pig whole!

Most snakes live on the land, but some live in trees and others in the water.

All snakes are good hunters. They must be, in order to live. Instead of eating grass, fruit, roots, or vegetables, small snakes eat grasshoppers, beetles, and other bugs and insects. Large snakes eat mice and rats. Still bigger ones eat squirrels and rabbits. The huge snakes could eat a small deer if they could catch one. Some snakes even eat other snakes.

There are biting snakes and squeezing snakes. Some snakes catch their food by biting it. Others catch it by wrapping themselves around it and squeezing it. Snakes don't chew their food. They just swallow it whole. After they have eaten, some snakes rest for two or three days.

Snakes aren't the only hunters, of course. At the same time *they* are hunting, some other animals are hunting them.

There are snakes that eat birds and the eggs of birds. And there are birds that eat snakes, too. Eagles, hawks, owls, and other large birds are among the worst enemies that snakes have. The big birds dive from the sky silently and swiftly to catch a snake before it knows the bird is there. Wild hogs catch snakes by stamping on them, and then they eat them.

The greatest snake fighter of all is probably a thick-furred little animal called a *mongoose*. It can move so fast that it can jump back from the strike of a giant cobra snake and then jump in and kill the cobra. If you live where cobras live, it is a good thing to have a mongoose for a pet.

Some of the greatest snake fighters are snakes themselves. Farmers and other persons who live in places where there are poisonous snakes like to have king snakes and black snakes near their houses. The king snakes and black snakes kill or chase away poisonous snakes.

If you go where snakes are: WATCH OUT . . . BE CAREFUL! It's true that many snakes won't hurt you. But other snakes are dangerous. Some even have needlelike fangs in their mouths. The fangs could punch holes in your skin if a snake bit you, and put poison into your blood. The poison is so bad that it can kill people.

So if you are in snake country, don't reach under a log or a rock.

If you are walking through bushes or brush, carry a stick to poke ahead of you. The movement and sound will usually frighten away any snake that might be there.

Most people who are bitten by snakes are bitten in the leg below the knee. So if you wear high boots in snake country, they will be a great protection.

Don't go wading or swimming in water where poisonous snakes are known to live.

Among the most dangerous snakes are rattlesnakes. They have rattles on the ends of their tails. They shake the rattles when they are alarmed. Rattles sound a little like pebbles being shaken fast in a wooden box. If you ever hear this sound, move away quickly.

Most snakes don't rattle—not even all rattlesnakes do. So when you are in snake country: WATCH OUT . . . BE CAREFUL.

You can learn about the snake-fighting Mongoose *in Volume 10 and about hibernation in Volume 1 under* Animals— "The Special Long Sleep."

Hello, Snow

You are looking out the window of your warm house. The sky is colorless and cold. It looks as if it would ring and clang if you could raise your fist and knock on it. The wind blows. The sun is hiding. What an unfriendly day! You turn away from the window.

An hour later your mother says, "Come look out the window!"

You wonder what there is to see that wasn't there before. You wonder why it's so quiet. The sounds of the city—voices, engines, alarms, wheels, horns—are hushed. When you look out the window, you see why. It's snowing. The snow has made a brand-new world, clean and soft and silent.

98

As snowflakes fall from the sky, they look like feathers, bits of lace, silvery spider webs, chips from a diamond. . . .

It's easy to catch a snowflake, but keeping one is harder. Snowflakes melt so fast. Take a piece of black paper or cloth outside with you to catch and hold a few snowflakes. And take a magnifying glass to get a really good look.

At first glance all snowflakes look the same. That's because they all have six sides. A closer look will show you that they are not the same—every one is different.

Aren't they pretty? How would you like to have your room wallpapered with pictures of snowflakes? Every night when you went to bed, you could have your own private snowstorm.

99

Can you imagine snow almost every night? That's a lot of snow.
But there are places where there is that much snow. Eskimos, who
live far north, toward the bitterly cold North Pole, have that
much snow. They have so much they can even make houses of it!

Even if it doesn't snow enough where you live to build a snowhouse, perhaps there will be enough snow to make a fort or a
snowman.

When it's very, very cold, the snow is as dry and unstickable as
sand. It won't pack in your hands to make a snowball. But just
wait until the sun comes out and softens the snow a little.

Then . . .

Look out, boys and girls! Here come the snowballs!

Snowballs come from boys and girls. Snowflakes come from the sky—from the billions of tiny water droplets up there that form clouds.

Sometimes the wind blows these clouds from a warm place to a very cold place. If the wind stops blowing, it leaves the clouds hanging in the freezing cold. When that happens, the tiny droplets of water in the cloud freeze into tiny ice crystals. And these ice crystals make up snowflakes.

Down
   down
     down
       comes the downy snow.

If you're interested in building a snowhouse, read Eskimos *in Volume 5.*
Are you interested in other kinds of weather? Look under Rain *in Volume 13 and* Weather *in Volume 16.*

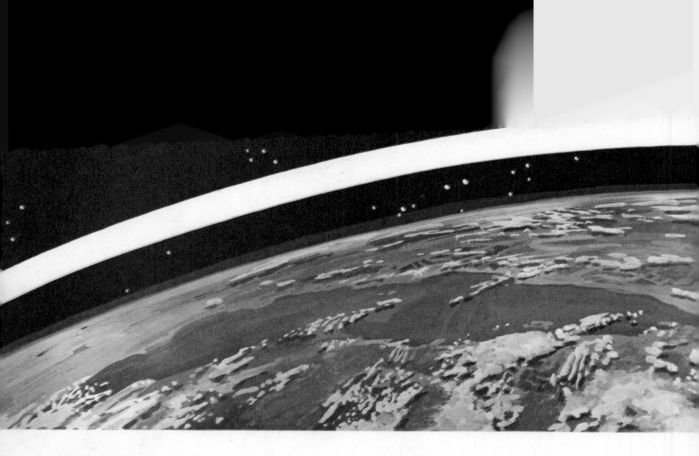

Thinking Fast

A space capsule travels very fast. It travels so fast that it can go all the way across the country from one ocean to the other while you are eating your breakfast.

When a space capsule is going around the Earth at this great speed—perhaps at 20,000 miles an hour—it takes fast thinking to steer it exactly where it should go.

People can't think that fast.

By the time you could think, "Now I'll turn the capsule," you would already be past the turning place! That is why one of the most important members of a space team is a machine called the *computer*.

The computer stays down on the ground, and as soon as a rocket fires, the computer starts working. It gets messages from the capsule *every second*. The computer knows exactly where the capsule is all the time.

If the capsule should go off its course, the computer can figure out what should be done to get the capsule back where it belongs. An instant message makes a rocket fire to steer the capsule back to where it ought to be.

With the computer figuring things out, second by second, the capsule can circle the Earth many times and then splash down safely in the ocean very close to the ship that will pick up the astronaut and capsule.

It might sound as if the computer were kept very busy, but for a computer it's not busy at all. Some of today's computers can figure out over a *million* things every *second!*

Sounds like a good machine to have on your team, doesn't it? And wouldn't it be handy to have a pocket computer at school to do your arithmetic problems?

Even though the computer can work out problems so fast, it doesn't really think. Men figure things out much more slowly, but men figured out how to make computers!

Want to know more?
Look up Astronauts *in Volume 1*
and Computers *in Volume 3.*

How Space Stations Will Be Used

Barroooommmm!

This is a "space bus" blasting off. The astronauts and space workers in this giant capsule are going to different places in space. But they start off together.

Why?

The hardest part of a space trip is getting the rocket and capsule up off the ground. It takes a lot of fuel and many men working on the ground to get the rocket and capsule up through the air and away from the Earth.

Once the spacecraft is far away from the Earth, it takes very little fuel to make it move.

Some of the things mentioned in this imaginary space story could happen today.

The rest may happen by the time you have grown up.

If three space teams are going to three different places—let's say the moon, a space lab, and another planet—there's no reason to waste fuel by blasting *three* rockets into space.

The teams can be blasted into space together to a special space station—a waiting station.

The waiting station, far out in space, where the space bus stops, has the things that people need to live. It has food, water, oxygen, toilets, and beds. It also has many of the things a waiting room at a bus or train station or airport on Earth would have.

The men who are going on the long space trip will wait at the waiting station for their special outer-space ship.

This ship will be delivered from another space station—the space garage. The space garage has room for many spaceships.

Before the spaceship is delivered, the space garage men put into it all the supplies needed for the long trip. The supplies have come from another space station, the space storehouse.

Whenever the storehouse needs more supplies, a large capsule filled with supplies, a "space freighter," will be rocketed from Earth to the storehouse.

Someday spaceships may be put together in a space-station factory.

Another group that came from Earth in the space bus are scientists. Soon the laboratory bus will pick them up. This bus runs back and forth between the waiting station and the laboratory station.

The workers bound for the moon will wait for the moon bus. The moon bus and the laboratory bus do not go to Earth. They just go back and forth between the waiting station and the moon or the laboratory.

The space bus that came from the Earth will be checked by garage men before it returns to Earth, just as on Earth airplanes are checked before each trip.

When it is ready to return, people from the moon bus and the laboratory bus who want to go back to Earth, will get aboard and the return trip will begin.

If you liked this story,
you'll like Astronauts *in Volume 1*.

The Spinning Spider

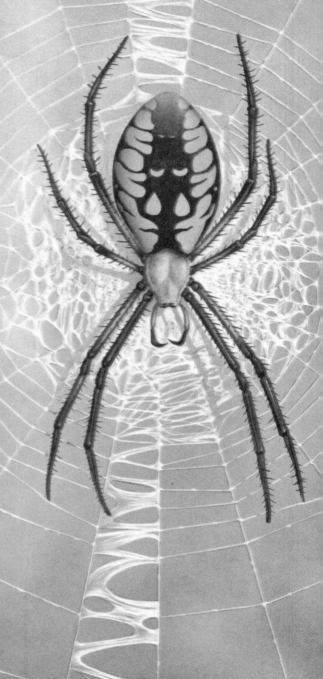

"Won't you come into my parlor?" said the spider to the fly.

Sitting on a soft cushion of silk in its web, this *golden garden spider* will wait . . . and wait . . . and wait. A breeze might sway the lacy nest, but this won't bother the spider.

Food is what this remarkable creature is waiting for so patiently. When a bug gets caught in the web, then the spider will move. Before a bug has time to do more than wiggle and squirm, the spider will rush out and spin some threads of silk around it to hold it tight and then crawl back to its soft, silken pillow to wait again.

Not all spiders make webs to catch food. Some, such as the *jumping spider,* pounce like a cat to capture insects. The big *wolf spider* chases insects on its long, spindly legs. The little *crab spider* hides between flower petals and grabs the insects that come to find nectar.

110

All spiders spin silk. They have a special spinning "factory" under their stomachs. With their *spinnerets*—which look like short fingers—they spin silk from a watery stuff that comes out through small holes. When it touches the air, the liquid silk changes into silk thread.

For lining their nests and for their webs, spiders spin strong, smooth silk. For trapping food in their webs, they spin sticky silk. Some spiders spin little bags of soft, fluffy silk to hold the eggs from which new spiders are born.

And suppose a spider is hurrying to escape from an enemy. It quickly spins a getaway thread to climb down on and then scurries away.

Spiders don't fly in airplanes when they want to take a trip. But some will climb to the tip of a leaf or a blade of grass, spin some threads, and wait for the wind to pick them up as if they were bits of dandelion fluff. The spiders float with the silken threads over fields and trees. When they come down, maybe they will be in a place where there are more flies and insects to catch.

Except in icy places or on high mountaintops, spiders live everywhere—even under the ground and under the water.

One underwater spider swims to the bottom of a pond or a stream and builds a silk house shaped like a thimble. It stores food there and the eggs that will hatch into new *water spiders*.

But the water spider can't breathe under water the way a fish can. It has to breathe the same kind of air that other spiders do—the same kind that *you* do.

Do you think it finds this air under the water?

It doesn't. It swims to the top of the water and brings air down in bubbles. It puts the bubbles of air in its underwater house. Then, whenever the spider wants to stay under the water a long time, it goes into its house and breathes the air it carried down in bubbles.

Furry, brown wolf spiders don't build a web or even a nest. They hide under leaves and grass. The mother spider drags her silken bag full of spider eggs with her wherever she goes. When the eggs hatch, the newborn babies climb onto her back and stay there until they can take care of themselves.

Spiders have eight legs. If they lose a leg, most spiders can grow a new one! Some spiders have as many as eight eyes. Some have one kind of eyes for seeing in the daytime and a different kind for seeing at night.

The biggest spider is bigger than your hand. Much bigger. Big enough to eat a bird! That's what it's called—a *bird spider*. Surprising as it might seem, this giant of the spiders isn't very dangerous to people. When bothered, it pinches a little with its mouth, but that's about all. Some people even keep it for a pet.

Spiders help us by destroying many harmful insects. And some spiders build beautiful webs. Most spiders won't hurt us. But a few will.

The *black widow spider* is little and shiny and black. It has a tiny, bright red mark on it. It lives under stones or under the bark of a tree or wherever it's dark and damp. It has a dangerous, poisonous bite.

The *brown recluse spider* is small, too. It has a dark, violin-shaped spot on its head. But the spot is hard to see, and the brown spider looks very much like some other spiders. It spins its web in warm, dry places, such as attics or barns, and it is almost as dangerous as the black widow spider.

The *tarantula* can hurt you if it bites you. It looks frightening because it is very big. It's scary and hairy. But its bite is not nearly so dangerous as that of the black widow spider or the brown spider.

Plant or Animal?

Did you ever take a bath with a skeleton? Or see somebody wash a car with one? Maybe you did!

There's something different about this sponge. It looks a little shaggy and ragged—not like the nice, neat man-made sponges you usually see. And it feels a little hard and tough.

It's this way because it is a skeleton—a skeleton of a creature that once lived in the ocean.

Sponges are strange animals. They don't have heads or tails or legs. They don't run or climb, as dogs and cats do. They just stay still and grow, as trees and cabbages do.

They even look more like a growing plant than like an animal. When they are young, they attach themselves to a rock or a coral reef in the ocean and stay in that same place for the rest of their lives.

In what parts of the world can sponges be found? Some are found along the coast of Florida. Let's go there to see.

First we have to get on a boat.
Now we are out on the ocean.
Where are the sponges?

Down there! Down in the
ocean. These sponge divers go
down to pick them. It's almost
as if they were picking flowers in
a garden. Afterward the sponges
are cleaned and trimmed and
sent to the market.

Although most sponges grow
in the ocean, you can sometimes
find little ones growing in freshwater—on a stick or a rock in a
pond or stream or ditch.

Not all sponges are very
spongy. Some are soft and
squishy. Some sponges have
skeletons almost like glass.
Sometimes they look like beautiful vases. They come in many
shapes and sizes and colors. But
they all hold water . . . until you
squeeze it out.

Did you like this story?
You'll want to read about Coral
in Volume 3 and Moss *in Volume 10.*

Spring in the Country

Spring in the country is the time when a million new neighbors arrive.

The first ones to arrive that I know about are the little frogs that we call *spring peepers*. They're not at all quiet or secretive. They sound like little tin whistles that can be heard for half a mile.

The peepers spend the winter at the bottom of our pond, with its soft, cozy mud wrapped around them like a blanket. They stay down there until something—I don't know exactly what—tells them that spring has come.

So the peepers crawl up the banks of the pond and start singing *Reeep-reeep-reeep!* Their song is beautiful because it says, "Spring has come!"

But most of our new neighbors are here before I know about it! They move in lightly on feathery wings or push their way up from the ground as quietly as shadows.

I didn't even know that these two little wrens lived right next door until I saw the brand-new house they'd built from twigs and grass.

I wonder how a flower sounds when it's unfolding. Not crackly like paper. Not squeaky like hinges. The purr of a cat? That's probably how a flower sounds when it spreads out its petals.

If you think I'm exaggerating about how many new neighbors we have, just look at the masses of flowers swinging from our lilac bushes.

And the ivy laddering its way up to my window.

121

There's one of the skunks that dozed under the floor of our barn all winter. It's on its way to go out visiting. While we're sleeping, it will probably raid our trash can, the way it did all last spring. It doesn't know that this year we have a new one. The top won't come off unless you twist it just so. You might say that wasn't very neighborly of us. But there are plenty of grubs and grasshoppers and other pests on this farm for the skunk to eat. That's why we let it and its family live here—rent free.

Besides, Mom and I think skunks are cute and fun to watch. Dad says, "I could get along without them!" Mom feels that way about the garter snakes. And I'd just as soon there weren't any mosquitoes.

Oh, well—when you've got a million neighbors, there are sure to be some you don't like. . .

and others that are just perfect!

Spring in the City

One morning late in March, the air feels as soft and warm as fur. It melts the patches of worn-out snowstorms into bright black puddles. They smile back at me.

Then the spring wind blows cool. *Wham!* It pushes me back when I try to turn the corner.

It shrieks, "Go away, warm weather! You can't bring summer yet. Not yet."

Torn paper, bits of plastic, peelings, lost mittens, jacks, jump ropes, dead leaves, weeds, dull ribbons—all lie in a heap at the bottom of the street. The city workers come to sweep them up . . . and sweep and sweep.

When it's springtime in the city, the weather is always changing. It can't make up its mind between summer and winter. I never know whether to wear my sweater or my coat.

The spring winds blow the sweepings around and around, teasing the workers.

Inside our apartment, Mom is busy taking down the curtains to wash them—*spring cleaning,* as she calls it. Mrs. Murphy next door is washing her windows, inside and out, and my sister is washing ours. Soon the winter's dirt is polished away, and I can see outside almost as if there were no window glass at all. And then it rains!

When the storm is over, I put on my rubber boots and run an errand for Mom. The streets and buildings are dark and wet against the deep blue evening sky.

I pretend I am the discoverer of a kingdom hidden under the sea.

124

The next morning it's the sun's turn. It dries off the damp streets and swallows the soft little puddles. It wakes up the seeds of trees and grass.

It wakes up the people, too. Big and bold, the sun will make another warm spring day. I help Dad stir the paint that he's going to use on the front door.

Pretty soon, up and down every street, people are scraping and painting, digging and planting, polishing and pounding. They're working as hard as spring itself to get the city ready for company.

Who is this company? I spent a long time wondering about that. And I finally figured it out. The company is anybody who takes the time to enjoy the city, all shining and beautiful in the springtime.

The Animal That Plants Trees

Who argues with the blue jays,
jumps from one tip-top tree branch
to another tip-top tree branch,
and runs around with its cheeks
filled with nuts?
The squirrel, of course.

Can you see its parachute? And
its umbrella? Can you find the
extra blanket it's carrying?

Sure you can. Its parachute is its tail. When it makes long jumps from branch to branch, it uses its tail to slow itself down in the air and to help itself land on its feet if it falls from a high place.

Its tail is also its umbrella when it rains.

And when it's cold—well, it uses its tail for a blanket.

It even has other uses for its tail. The squirrel has many enemies, and it protects itself with its tail when it fights.

Chatter-chatter-chatter. Who's making all that noise?

A father squirrel is warning all the animals to stay away from his and mother squirrel's new babies sleeping in the nest. When they can't find a hollow tree, squirrels carry sticks and leaves and build nests in high tree branches. The father squirrel stays outside the nest, looking and listening and sniffing as he guards his family from animals that would like to steal his babies and eat them.

There are so many kinds of squirrels—gray squirrels, red squirrels, white squirrels, fox squirrels, ground squirrels, and flying squirrels. Watch them chase one another up and down tree trunks—along electric-light wires—up and down the sides of buildings—and over the rooftops. Watch them hide nuts and pinecones in hollow trees or dig holes and bury them under the ground.

Because they live most of their lives in trees, baby squirrels must learn such things as how to walk headfirst down a tree and how to jump from one branch to another branch without falling. Then, someday, their mother will take them down the tree trunk and teach them how to find mushrooms and grasshoppers to eat without being caught by a hawk, a weasel, or a fox.

During the winter, when the ground is frozen or covered with snow, squirrels can eat the food they stored away. Nobody knows for sure how they find the nuts they bury. Maybe they smell them. Maybe they can see where the ground has been dug up a little. Squirrels in an oak or walnut forest bury so many nuts that it seems that they could dig almost anywhere and find an acorn or walnut.

Some of the hidden nuts are never found, and many grow to become trees. Squirrels are a great help in keeping our forests growing. They plant more trees than almost anybody.

To learn how most squirrels spend their winters, read "The Special Long Sleep" *under* Animals *in Volume 1.*

STORKS

The Bird on Your Chimney

Children in the northern part of the United States wait for the robin to come in the spring. Children in the northern countries of Europe wait for a bird much bigger than a robin—almost a hundred times bigger. Its long, thin legs make it about as tall as you!

This bird is a stork.

There is a very special thing about storks. These great big birds like to build their nests on top of people's houses.

Some people think it's good luck for you if a stork builds its nest on top of your house. Maybe it is, because storks *do* help keep rats and mice and little snakes away from backyard gardens.

A story as old as the Santa Claus story says that storks bring the new babies to people's houses and drop them down the chimneys into the waiting arms of mothers. Storks don't, of course. It's only a *pretend* story. But storks *are* gentle and friendly creatures that seem to like to live close to people.

Storks fly a long way across water and land to get where they are going. They fly so high in the air that you can barely see them. But you can *hear* them.

Since storks are silent and never sing, do you wonder how people can hear them? When you are happy, you clap your hands. Go ahead—do it. And listen when you do. That's the kind of happy clapping sound that storks make. They click their long red bills while they are flying. The sound floats down from the sky as the many beautiful white storks and a few black ones fly along on their great flapping wings, with their long legs hanging down behind them.

Two at a time, storks come down from the sky to housetops, where they will build their nests.

It would be hard for storks to build their big, round nest on a sharp roof. So the children of the house beg their father to put a large wheel on the housetop or even on the chimney. The storks go to work at once building their large, messy nest by weaving sticks and straw in and out of the wheel spokes. Then they rest.

What do you do when you want to rest? Sit down? Lie down? Squat? Storks rest by standing on one leg! How long can you stand on one leg? Storks stand that way for hours and never look tired!

The mother stork lays eggs and then kicks one egg out of the nest. Why? Only the stork knows, but people try to guess. Some say that she is paying her rent for the use of the wheel. Children watch and wait, hoping to catch the egg as it falls. Usually they miss.

After the young storks are born, the children gather to watch the baby storks' first wobbly steps on the sharp rooftop. The young storks grow fast all summer, and when autumn is near, they start exercising to get their wings strong for the long flight south.

The storks stay away all winter, but in the spring they come clapping back to the northern countries, where happy children wait for them, hoping the big birds will again build nests on their rooftops.

If you liked this article,
read about Birds *in Volume 2.*

Strange Music

People said that Igor Stravinsky was going to be a famous musician. Then he wrote a piece called *The Rite of Spring*.

Most people who heard it the first time it was played thought the music was terrible. They booed and stamped their feet. Some threw things at the orchestra.

The music *was* different. It sounded strange—not like the music people were used to hearing.

Even when he was a child in Russia, Igor experimented with music. He took piano lessons, but he was always making up his own music instead of playing notes the way they were written.

His teacher didn't approve. "Please!" he said. "Play the notes the way they are written or your music will never amount to anything."

Igor's father encouraged his son to become a lawyer.

Igor tried. He studied to become a lawyer. But he never stopped writing music. A good friend introduced his father, the great Russian composer Rimski-Korsakov, to Igor. After that, instead of writing music just for the piano, Igor began to write for all the instruments in the orchestra.

It took a long time, but Stravinsky's music did become popular. He wrote compositions for ballet dancers, as well as for musicians. He became so popular that many composers have tried to write music the way he did. Today people do not say Igor Stravinsky's music is terrible. Many even say it is wonderful.

You may read about other famous composers under Bach *and* Beethoven *in Volume 2 and* Mozart *in Volume 10.*

Summer in the Country

"In the summer the country has as many sounds as downtown."
That's what my cousin from the city said after I'd shown her
around the farm. I'd always thought the country was much
quieter than the city . . . until I tried listening to it the way a
city person might.

And you know what? My cousin was right! The country is crowded with noises in summer.

I didn't have to listen very closely to hear Dad's tractor huffing and puffing and *put-putting* in the cornfield. Dad's tractor is stronger than a whole team of horses, and it pulls the big farm machines that look like monsters wearing coats of armor. But you don't need to be afraid of these machines. They're really very good machines. Many of them can do as much work in an hour as a man can do in a *week!*

At noontime I heard the old bell ring. The bell is on a pole that stands outside the kitchen door. Mom rings the bell to signal Dad when lunch is ready or when he's wanted on the telephone or when company comes. The bell goes *clang-clang-clang*. You can hear it anywhere on the farm.

I kept listening for sounds all during lunch, and afterward while Dad was stretched out on a cot in the shade of the porch. He always rests there for a while in the summer . . . until the red-hot sun has lowered and the day has cooled a bit.

I heard the chickens singsonging.

Cluck-cluck-cluck.

I wonder what that means. I hope it's something good because chickens *cluck-cluck-cluck* about three million times a day. I hope it means "yes" or "beautiful" or "okay."

Toward evening I brought the cows in from the pasture to the barn. They sounded like a bunch of friends trying to remember the tune of a song. *Moo,* one cow began in a very deep voice. Another cow shook her head and *mooed* in a higher voice. Pretty soon they were all *mooing,* and no two sounded exactly alike!

Usually in the summer, after doing chores all day, I fall asleep the minute I jump into bed. But that night, when I was listening to the country the way a city person might, I stayed wide awake.

I listened to the moths thumping and bumping on the window screen like acrobats.

I heard a whine as the wind turned the rusty blades on the windmill. The wind was scolding, "Get to work—don't just stand still. Pump, pump, pump the water."

From the fields came the beep of the cicadas. They're great big black and green insects that call to one another from the trees. They sound like the busy signal on the telephone.

Loudest of all were the singing crickets and the tree frogs. They never stopped—even for a tiny second.

The next thing I heard were the roosters—ours and our neighbors'. I think roosters have the best job in the world. They announce the sunrise. When the dark sky turns golden, the roosters flap their wings and sing:

Cock-a-doodle-doo!
The night is over.
The day is new!

Summer in the City

When it's summer in the city, it always seems that nobody's home. There might as well not be any roofs or walls. People don't seem to want them. Everybody's roof is the light blue sky. There might as well not be telephones or doorbells, either, because people are hardly ever there to answer them. The only way to find your friends is to go looking for them.

There are several places where I usually can find one or more of my friends.

If there's a man on a corner with a suitcase full of toys that do tricks, I nearly always find one of my friends watching him as he slowly w-i-n-d-s them up and, *zing,* lets them go!

And I always check the hot-dog stand in the park. It smells so nice and spicy you almost sneeze when you get close.

I look for my friends at the big fountain, too. A little old lady comes there every single morning at 11 o'clock with a big sack of bread for the pigeons. Hundreds of them come flying.

On hot afternoons my friends play tag in the tall, cool shadows of Abraham Lincoln. From what I've heard about him, I'd guess he'd like us to be playing there.

One hot day I found my friend Roger sitting on the muddy banks of the park lagoon with a fishing pole in his hand.

"I'll bet you don't catch any fish in there," I said.

"I'll bet I don't care," said Roger. "It's so hot, I'd rather have a fish catch *me!*"

We all go home to eat supper, but as soon as it's over, we're all back out again. We sit on the front steps of our buildings and watch the parade of people.

There are miles and miles of people. They walk by slowly, looking at us looking at them. There are lots of cheery hellos and so longs and laughing.

Some of the people are all dressed up to go somewhere special. Others are in their everyday clothes. They're just out because it's too nice to be in.

When sunset finally comes, it tints all the buildings rose and orange and gold. And it also makes the people—dressed up or not—look colorful.

But the nicest thing of all about summer is how it gets people to go outdoors.

Tim, the Spaceman

When Tim was six years old he built his first spaceship. The outer shell was a tall trash can that Tim had very carefully hosed out. Inside there was a tall stool for Tim to sit on as he guided the ship higher and higher—farther and farther into outer space.

There was lots of good junk in the trash can that Tim turned into instruments for his spaceship. There was an alarm clock with no face, but a loud bell that rang and rang. An old radio had several dials that turned this way and that way very nicely, even though there were no tubes or anything behind them. There was a rusty chain, good and long, that Tim tied a rock to and used as an anchor.

"What is that?" asked Tina, who was Tim's twin sister.

"It's a spaceship," Tim said as he swung himself over the side and onto the stool. "I'm going to ride up to the sun in it."

"Good-bye—have a nice trip!" called Tina, as she started down the block toward her friends who were jumping rope.

Just then the mailman came by. "What are you up to, Tim?" he asked.

"I'm getting my spaceship ready for a trip to the sun," Tim said.

"Are you planning to go all by yourself?"

"Of course," Tim said. "Why not?"

"Well, you might get kind of lonesome. The sun is almost a hundred million miles away. That's a long, long trip to take all by yourself." The mailman hitched his bag higher on his shoulder. "If I were you, I'd ask somebody to come along with me."

143

Tim sat there thinking. When he saw the boy who lived in the next house, he shouted at him, "Want to ride up to the sun with me in my spaceship?"

"No thanks," said the boy.

"Why not?" Tim asked.

"Because I don't want to get blinded. The sun is really a shining star. Even here on Earth the sun is so bright that it will hurt your eyes if you look straight at it very long."

"Are you sure?"

"I'm positive," the boy said. "We studied about the sun at school. You shouldn't look at the sun."

"I'm sorry you won't come," said Tim. "But thanks for telling me about the sun. I'll remember not to look at it."

"Hey, Otto!" Tim called to his friend the paper boy. "Why don't you come up to the sun with me in my spaceship?"

"I'm afraid I'd get lost up there," Otto said. "The sun is a big, *big* place."

"It doesn't look that big," Tim said.

"The sun is more than a million times bigger than the Earth," Otto told him. "It doesn't look that big because it's so far away— almost a hundred million miles from where we're standing."

"I know," Tim said. "That's just what the mailman told me." He waved good-bye as Otto pedaled his bike down the street. "I wish I had someone to keep me company on such a long trip."

"Hi, Tim!" the delivery man called, as he reached for a box of groceries from the back of his truck. "What can I do for you today?"

"Why don't you come up to the sun with me on my spaceship?"

"I don't think I'd like it on the sun," the delivery man said.

"Why not?"

"No place to put your feet down on the sun—that's why. The sun doesn't have rocks and sand and dirt on it."

"Well then, what does the sun have?" Tim asked. "It has to have something on it or else we wouldn't see it every day."

"The sun is fire. Nothing but fire—inside, outside, and all around."

"You mean the sun has no people or animals or plants anywhere?"

The delivery man shook his head. "Just fire."

"Ti-im!" It was his mother's voice.

"I've got to go now," Tim told the delivery man.

"Tim, I need to empty some things in the trash can. What have you done with it?" Tim's mother asked.

"I made it into a spaceship that would take me up to the sun," Tim said.

"I hope you plan to launch it soon," Tim's father said. "It's blocking the driveway. I had to park the car in the street."

"I'm not going to launch it," Tim said.

"Why not?" his father asked.

Tim took a deep breath, "Well, in the first place, the sun is millions and millions of miles away, and it would take too long to get there. And even if I did, I couldn't see where I was because the sun is so bright it would blind me. And there's no place to walk or sit down because the sun is all fire."

"And the fire of the sun is so hot that it would melt a spaceship before it even got there," Tim's father added. "But there are other places out in space."

"I'm going to find out everything about them," Tim said, "before I go to the trouble of building another spaceship."

"Now you're talking like a real spaceman!" his father said.

If you would like to find out other things about outer space before building a spaceship, look up Astronauts *in Volume 1 and* Space *in Volume 14.*

The Sun and Its Planets

This is a picture of the Earth. Not as we usually see it, because we see only a little bit of the Earth when we're looking from our houses or even from the top of a very tall building.

But this is how the Earth might look from far out in space—the way it looks to astronauts as they travel to the moon.

Here is another picture of the Earth. But this time it looks much smaller. If we traveled many millions of miles out into space—even farther than astronauts do—the Earth would appear this tiny.

This is how the Earth would look if we were many, many *millions* of miles out in space (it's the small ball with the arrow pointing to it). The sun looks about the size of a dime. And the round object with rings around it is Saturn. Saturn and Earth are *planets*. They move around the sun. There are seven other planets, too—nine all together. The sun and the planets are part of what is called the *solar system*.

Now, just suppose we could travel—not millions and millions of miles—but millions and millions and *millions* and *billions* of miles away from the Earth and the rest of our solar system.

Can you find the red arrow in this picture? It's pointing at a tiny star in the sky. That tiny star is what our sun would look like if we could travel all those millions and billions of miles. The Earth and all the other planets would be so small that you couldn't even see them!

Imagine being so far from home and seeing that small star that is our sun and saying,

> Star light,
> Star bright,
> First star I see tonight. . . .

Want to know more?
Look up Astronauts *in Volume 1,*
Moon *in Volume 10, and* Space
in this book.

More About the Sun

All the big planets in our solar system travel around the sun at different speeds. As they move in their paths, or *orbits,* around the sun, the planets also spin around like tops.

As the Earth spins, the part of it that faces the sun has daylight. The part that faces away from the sun has night. (When it's day in New York City, it's night in Tokyo, Japan.)

As far as we know, there are no living things on any planet except Earth, though no one can say for certain. The Earth's distance from the sun gives our planet exactly the amount of heat and light that plants and animals need for life. If you look carefully at the picture, you'll be able to see which planet is closest to the sun. It's *Mercury*

Venus is the brightest planet and is sometimes called the *evening star.*

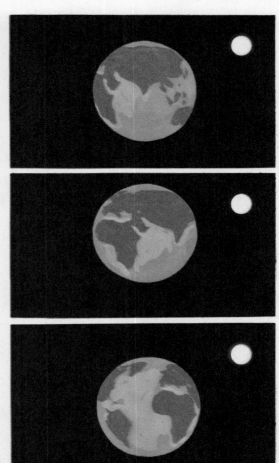

On certain nights you can see the planet *Mars,* which looks something like a red star in the sky.

Jupiter is the largest planet.

Saturn has three rings around it, which are made of many bits, or *particles.*

Uranus is visible only when the skies are very clear.

Neptune is so far from the sun—and so dark—that we can't see it without a telescope.

Pluto is farthest away from the sun.

When we have learned more about our solar system and space travel, we may be able to visit other planets.

Anyone for a trip to Mars?

If you liked this story, you'll like "Life on Other Planets" *under* Life *in Volume 9.*

Let's Take a Walk Under the Ocean

He is not a man from outer space! This is an earthman ready to dive down into the mysterious waters that make up more than half of our world. People who dive this way are called *scuba divers*.

So that they can breathe under water and move around faster, most deep-sea divers wear what the man in the picture is wearing.

The scuba diver wears a face mask. It has a circle of clear glass through which he can see. The glass, in a rubber frame, has a

band that fits closely around the diver's head so that no water can seep in.

The scuba diver wears a tank on his back. In this tank is all the air he will need to breathe for an hour or more while he is under water. The air goes into his mouth through a tube from the tank.

When a scuba diver dives, a rubber suit keeps the cold water out and the heat of his body in.

On his feet, the scuba diver wears long, flat shoes made of rubber. They are called fins, because they look very much like the fins of real fish. The diver's fins help him to swim and turn faster.

If you were a scuba diver, what would you do under the water?

You might carry an underwater camera and take color pictures of the beautiful fish that most people never get to see.

Some scuba divers search for treasure. They dive into places where they think pirate ships might have been sunk.

Many scuba divers like to dive under water just for the joy of seeing the strange and beautiful things that are down there. In places it is almost like a fairy-tale world, with lacy coral rock in the shape of castles and arches. Fish swim slowly past your face. Little fish and big fish. Fish striped like zebras. Fish spotted like giraffes. Gold, blue, and red fish, and every other color you can think of. Tall sea grasses bend and ripple under the water.

When you are older and have passed all the swimming tests, do you want to be a scuba diver? You will probably start out as a skin diver, with just a face mask. First you will probably explore the bottom of a swimming pool.

After you have learned how to use your face mask, you will get a pair of fins for your feet. With your face down, you will look into the waters of a small lake or pond, while your kicking feet move you lazily around.

After much practice, you will be ready to strap on a tank of air, or *aqualung,* and dive down under the water from a boat. Then you will see for yourself the wonderful world down there.

If you liked this story,
you'll want to read all about Aquanauts *in Volume 1.*

Where Am I?

Hans lives in a country that is more than half covered by high, steep mountains. From the window of his house he can see their peaks. The mountains are so high that the railroad train running between them looks like a toy.

In winter Hans's father puts stones on top of their house to keep the winter wind from blowing the roof off! Sometimes Hans has to ski to school because the roads are blocked with snow. Long ago, big Saint Bernard dogs used to rescue people who were lost in snowstorms in these mountains.

When spring comes, the warm wind often melts the snow too fast, and it comes sliding down the mountainside faster than an express train, and roaring like a zoo full of lions. This is called an *avalanche,* and it can be very dangerous.

Visitors from many countries come here for mountain climbing and for skiing and skating. These visitors buy souvenirs in the shops—cuckoo clocks or carved animals or music boxes. Some buy chocolate or cheese with big holes in it.

In the summer Hans practices blowing the *alphorn*. This is a wooden horn so long that one end rests on the ground. Hans's uncle teaches him to yodel. *Yodeling* is a special kind of singing— you have to do tricks with your voice.

Have you guessed the name of the country where Hans lives? The people are called Swiss, but they don't speak Swiss. They speak French or German or Italian.

The name of their country is Switzerland—a land of winter snow and summer meadows in the high beautiful mountains.

Look under Where Am I? *in Volume 16 and find Switzerland on the map.*

Credits

Pages	Art	Text
6-9	Ruth	Johnson
10-11	D'Achille	Johnson
12-13	Pulver	A. Reeve
14-19	Brusstar	Johnson
20-25	Mill	Zucker
26-31	Liese	Dennis
32-33	Taylor	Roginski
34-37	Wills	A. Reeve
38-41	Haesly	Stevenson, Johnson
42-45	Wills	Johnson
46-49	C. Amundson	Zucker
50-51	Fairbairn	Johnson
52-57	Kane	Nims
58-61	Shires	Stevenson
62-65	Kane	Nims
66-75	Kane	Johnson
76-79	Kane	Zucker
80-81	Mariash	Dennis
82-83	Moser	Nims
84-87	Brusstar	Johnson
38-97	Huff	Zucker
98-101	O'Sullivan	Nims
102-109	Meyer	Dennis
110-115	Ebel	Zucker
116-119	Meighan	Engh
120-125	Sharpe	Nims
126-129	Wills	Scherbaum
130-133	Wills	Rabe
134-135	Aronson	Zucker
136-141	Sharpe	Nims
142-147	Shires	Dennis, Nims
148-153	Meyer	Zucker
154-157	Kane	Zucker
158-159	Kollar	Marko